HEADLINES!™

HEALTH CARE FOR EVERYONE

MOLLY JONES

ROSEN
PUBLISHING®

New York

Health Care for Everyone *is dedicated to Dr. Thomas R. (Bob) Scott for the valuable gift of his time and insights.*

Published in 2011 by The Rosen Publishing Group, Inc.
29 East 21st Street, New York, NY 10010

Library of Congress Cataloging-in-Publication Data

Jones, Molly, 1933–
Health care for everyone / Molly Jones.
    p. cm. — (Headlines!)
Includes bibliographical references and index.
ISBN 978-1-4488-1290-5 (library binding)
1. Medical care—United States. 2. Health care reform—United States.
3. Health services accessibility—United States. 4. Health insurance—United States.
I. Title.
RA395.A3J663 2011
362.10973—dc22

2010024137

Manufactured in Malaysia

CPSIA Compliance Information: Batch #W11YA: For further information, contact Rosen Publishing, New York, New York, at 1-800-237-9932.

On the cover: In March 2010, demonstrators in Washington, D.C., show support for President Barack Obama and his administration's historic health care reform bill, the Patient Protection and Affordable Care Act.

CONTENTS

I n most highly developed nations, health care for all has long been a reality. Germany's health care system, which covers all citizens, began in 1883. At first, Germany's system included low-income workers and some government employees. Then it gradually expanded to cover virtually the entire population. Today, German workers and their employers are required to contribute a percentage of their salaries to help pay for insurance for everyone.

Thirty-one countries make up the Organisation for Economic Co-operation and Development (OECD), including Australia, Canada, France, Germany, Japan, Norway, Sweden, the United Kingdom, and the United States. Of these nine, the United States is the only country without universal health care, or a health care system that serves all of the people. In the United States, health care for everyone is a divisive issue.

On March 23, 2010, President Barack Obama signed a major health care reform bill, known as the Patient Protection and Affordable Care Act, into law. The new plan aroused fiery debate in Congress and around the nation. The debate focused on many of the same issues that have been argued throughout the past century. Although many people

Joined by fellow Democrats, President Barack Obama signs the Patient Protection and Affordable Care Act on March 23, 2010, after a fourteen-month political battle.

claim the plan does not go far enough to solve the problems that plague health care, for the first time in history almost all Americans will be able to obtain some type of health insurance.

Access to health care when it is needed, as well as the quality of medical care available, is crucial to the health of our citizenry. To make good health care decisions both as a nation and as individuals, citizens need to understand what insurance is and how it works; how the rapid growth of technology is affecting health care; how the doctor-patient relationship is changing; and what America's health care future might hold. The nation's health care system is everybody's business.

CHAPTER 1

The Mounting Costs of Health Care

Health care and the practice of medicine in the United States today bear little resemblance to care and practice early in the twentieth century. Changes in how doctors conduct their practices and relate to their patients, new ways of diagnosing and treating health conditions, the rapid advancement of medical technology, and ballooning costs have created a different world for both doctors and patients.

Where Has the Community Doctor Gone?

Many grandparents today remember a doctor who made house calls. He (female doctors were rare) arrived at the home when a family member was very ill. Usually he carried a small black leather bag containing instruments he might use to examine the patient, along with an assortment of pills, tonics, and salves to begin treatment. Often the doctor was a longtime member of the community, and patients knew him as a personal friend.

As the twenty-first century began, however, the doctor-patient relationship had become very different. According to data reported by the Kaiser Family Foundation in 2005, the average time a family

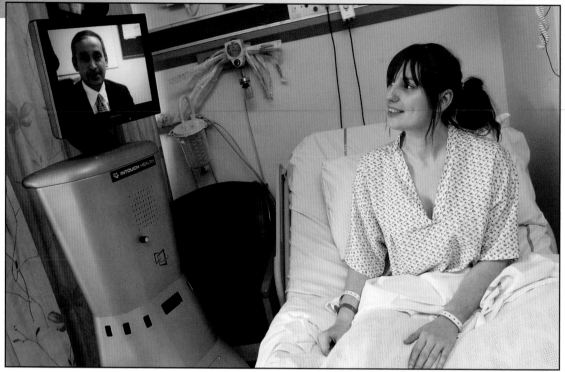

Doctors at St. Mary's Hospital in London, England, use remote presence robots to assist them in examining and communicating with patients.

doctor spends with a patient during an office visit today is about sixteen minutes. With the number of patients most doctors now see in a day, house calls would be impossible.

In fact, technology can now perform many of a doctor's functions. Sometimes it is possible for a patient to be diagnosed and treated without seeing a doctor at all. In some cases, remote medical technology can replace the need for a helicopter flight to a distant hospital. Data obtained with instruments can be transmitted instantly via computer, radio, or telephone. Doctors may even view the patient's body by television or Internet transmission and then give instructions to those attending the patient.

In rural or remote areas, such as northern Alaska, the nearest doctor may be hundreds of miles away. Because of advances in technology, vital information about the patient can be obtained on-site with special instruments and transmitted electronically to a distant medical center. There, specialists are able to analyze the information, make a diagnosis, and prescribe treatment. Patients may never see the remote doctor who diagnoses them.

THE GROWING ROLE—AND GROWING COST—OF TECHNOLOGY

Technology has made major changes in medical care, enabling faster and more accurate diagnosis and treatment. Tests of blood and other fluids, internal body scans, and devices that monitor organ functions can provide doctors with quick, precise information about the body's condition.

The emerging field of robotics has already affected the medical and surgical world, and its influence continues to grow. In a presentation to the Congressional Robotics Caucus in 2009, a single robotics company, daVinci, reported that through 2008 approximately three hundred thousand patients had received medical-surgical robotic procedures using its technology. The company projected that the number would grow to at least five hundred thousand within the next two years. Robots can perform or assist with surgeries by guiding and positioning instruments. They can also make other medical procedures, such as radiation therapy, more precise. In many procedures, the use of robotics may offer advantages over human performance, such as increased accuracy and reduced damage to body tissues.

In addition to improving medical outcomes, technology has enabled a single doctor to treat many more patients in a day. While one may think that the efficiency brought by technology would decrease medical costs, the high cost of technology has made the opposite true. According to a 2008 report by the Congressional Budget Office (CBO), in the past four decades the proportion of the national income devoted to health care has nearly tripled. The CBO estimates that about half of this immense growth in health care spending is associated with advances in technology.

Most doctors in earlier years were general practitioners, or primary care doctors. Now more and more physicians specialize in a narrow range of health problems, such as skin conditions (dermatology), cancer (oncology), digestive and intestinal disorders (gastroenterology), or heart and circulatory conditions (cardiology). In addition to affecting the doctor-patient relationship, specialization has added to patients' costs. When a primary care doctor sees a patient today, instead of treating a condition, the doctor may refer the patient to a specialist. The specialist will usually have more training than the primary care doctor in the special area of medicine. He or she will also have the most advanced technological equipment needed for that specialty.

A patient with more than one disorder may be seen and treated by a number of specialists in addition to the primary care doctor. According to the American Academy of Family Physicians (AAFP), the average cost of a visit with a specialist is greater than a visit with a primary care physician. In fact, the median income for doctors in some specialties is more than twice that of primary care doctors.

A further change in medical practice has affected both the doctor-patient relationship and the cost of care. For the past four decades, the percentage of doctors in solo or independent practices has declined. Instead, more and more doctors are joining group practices. For physicians, group practices have the advantage of shared technology and records. However, patients who are seen by different doctors on different visits sometimes lose the confidence and comfort of having a close connection with one doctor.

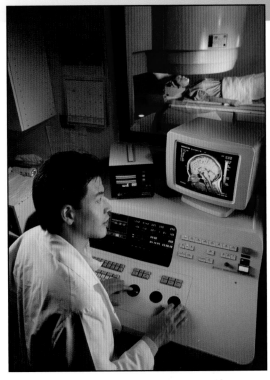

A medical technician uses magnetic resonance imaging (MRI) to produce computerized images of organs and tissues inside a patient's body. Technologies such as MRI assist doctors in diagnosing injuries and illnesses.

WHILE COSTS SOARED, AMERICANS LOST CARE

While recent changes in medicine have produced impressive health advances for Americans who could afford them, they have also brought skyrocketing costs. The high cost of treatment has prevented many people from getting the health care they need. Between 2000 and 2007, an estimated five million families filed for bankruptcy as a result of their medical expenses. Even more shocking, many of those who filed for bankruptcy had health insurance. Their plans simply didn't cover enough of their costs.

Though the United States has made great advances in medical science over the last century, the nation has fallen short in making medical care available to all citizens. In 2009, according to the Gallup-Healthways Well-Being Index, 16 percent of Americans had no health care insurance at all. The number of people in this situation has been rising in recent years.

The United States produces more goods and services each year than any other nation, and it spends a larger percentage of its national income on health than does any other nation. However, the health of Americans is far from the best. According to the British newspaper the *Guardian*, the average life expectancy of Americans at birth is equal to that of Cubans and lower than that of people in England, Japan, Italy, Germany, France, and Canada.

For more than a century, national leaders have wrestled with and disagreed about how to solve the problems of cost and access that burden America's health care system. In December 2009, the *New Yorker* reminded readers of the words of Irving Fisher, a Yale economist, who said, "At present the United States has the unenviable distinction of being the only great industrial nation without compulsory health insurance." The surprise is, Fisher made that speech in 1916.

That same year, the president of the American Medical Association (AMA), Dr. Rupert Blue, said, "Health insurance will constitute the next great step in social legislation." Fifty-three years later, as the discussion continued in 1969, Forrest Walker quoted Dr. Blue's words in the *Journal of American History*.

A Profile of Uninsured Americans Before the 2010 Legislation

All Americans were represented among those who had no health insurance prior to the 2010 health care legislation. However, Latinos, African Americans, and persons with low income were affected most. The table below shows what percentage of each population group had no health insurance in 2009.

Group	Percent Without Health Insurance
Hispanics or Latinos	41.5
Income < $36,000	28.6
Non-Hispanic Blacks	19.9
All Adults	16.0
All Americans (2007 Census)	15.3
Non-Hispanic Whites	11.6
Income $36,000-$89,999	8.8
Income $90,000+	3.6

Source: 2009 Gallup-Healthways Well-Being Index

In 1912, Theodore Roosevelt's campaign for president included support for health insurance in industry. In 1915, Progressives supported a plan for state-based compulsory health insurance. Some type of national health insurance plan has been proposed, argued, and defeated in almost every decade. Over the years, when polled, the American public has generally favored a national health plan but has disagreed in each case about how it should be financed and administered.

A Step Toward Health Care for Everyone

Debate and discussion about the nation's health care system is sure to continue, even though the 2010 health care legislation has become law. Some individuals and groups who opposed the health legislation have stated their intent to have the law repealed or declared unconstitutional.

Others still support ideas that were proposed but did not become part of the final plan. One of these ideas is universal health care, under which medical services would be equally available to all and would be funded by taxes. Another idea is a single payer plan, under which all medical bills would be paid by one government-run agency, rather than by the thousands of offices that now handle medical bills. A third idea is a public option, which would enable citizens who could not obtain private insurance to buy health insurance offered by the government.

Any of these plans would have been primarily a public, or government-based, way of expanding health care. Instead, the plan enacted by Congress increases the number of people insured by private health insurance companies. Whether one thinks health insurance should be mainly public or private depends on one's fundamental ideas about insurance. A look back at how insurance originated, how it works, and how it became so prominent in American life will help clarify many of the terms and concepts in the health care headlines.

CHAPTER 2

THE WHAT, WHY, AND HOW OF HEALTH INSURANCE

While legislators wrote and debated the health care over-haul, the language of insurance, especially health care insurance, peppered the news. Long before the 2010 legislation, however, insurance had become a key part of the way health care works in the United States.

WHAT IS INSURANCE?

The idea of insurance grew out of the natural ways people have pro-tected themselves from disaster throughout history. Ancient Chinese and Babylonian traders divided their goods among several ships so that if disaster struck one vessel, all would not be lost. Villagers in medieval Europe and in colonial America were quick to help neigh-bors rebuild a house after a fire. That way, they were ensured that neighbors would do the same for them if their house burned.

Centuries ago in England, shipowners insured themselves against sustaining a greater loss than they could afford. Each owner contrib-uted a set amount of money to a fund. The sum of the contributions

Settlers in colonial Massachusetts practiced an early form of insurance. People helped others rebuild their houses after a fire in order to be assured of help if they ever needed it.

was used to repair or replace any ships that were damaged or lost. This way, everyone paid a little and all were insured against a devastating loss. No individual had to bear all of the loss if disaster struck. The community or group shared the cost.

Modern health insurance is also a means of sharing risk. An unexpected illness, major surgery, injuries from an accident, or a catastrophic disease such as cancer may cost hundreds of thousands of dollars in doctor, hospital, and prescription drug bills. Few people can afford to pay such bills. However, when each person in a large group pays a moderate amount of money into a health insurance fund, the collected money can pay the huge bills of those unlucky enough to experience devastating health costs. Some nations pay for health care primarily through public health plans. In the United States, a combination of public and private health insurance is used.

Though both public and private insurance operate on the same principle of risk sharing that ancient cooperative plans did, other complex factors are involved. For example, private insurance is a profit-making business. Public insurance, on the other hand, is government-sponsored and funded through tax revenues or other assessments.

HOW DOES HEALTH INSURANCE WORK?

A health insurance policy is a legal contract between the insured person or group and the insurance provider (the company or agency that provides the insurance). The policy describes what the insurance will cover. It lists the exact illnesses, conditions, and circumstances for which the provider will award money, how much will be paid, and who will receive the money. For example, the money may be paid directly to the doctor or hospital, or it may be paid to the sick or injured person to reimburse health expenses. The policy also states the amount of money, or premium, the insured party must pay to get coverage.

The cost of an insurance policy is determined by estimating the risk, or probability, that a person will become ill or injured. It also takes into account how much these illnesses are likely to cost in doctor, hospital, prescription drug, and other medical services bills. For public

Health insurance policies specify which medical treatments and conditions are covered by the insurance and how much money can be awarded for each.

insurance, the estimated cost is paid by taxes, along with assessments from the insured individuals or their employers. For private insurance companies, which are profit-making businesses, the amount of profit the company expects to make is added to the projected expenses in order to calculate the premiums.

To make the most profit, health insurance providers attempt to insure many people with a low risk of illness. They also try to avoid insuring a large number of people at high risk. In the past, for example, companies have often refused to insure people with preexisting

WHAT THEY SAID ABOUT HEALTH CARE

While more and more Americans were losing health insurance, public figures, from presidents to news analysts, expressed a wide range of opinions about the need to improve America's health care system.

"Canada has shown the world how to balance freedom with compassion, and tradition with innovation, in your efforts to provide health care to all your citizens..." – Bill Clinton, 1995 address to Canada's House of Commons

"Our health care system is the envy of the world." – George W. Bush, 2004 presidential debate

"Without adequate health care, no one can make full use of his or her talents and opportunities." – Richard Nixon, 1974 address to U.S. Congress

"America's health care system is neither healthy, caring, nor a system." – Walter Cronkite, *CBS Evening News*

conditions. These are illnesses or medical conditions, such as cancer or diabetes, that the person already had before applying for health insurance. People with prior illnesses are almost certain to have greater medical expenses in the future than those without such conditions.

Many Americans have been denied health coverage altogether or had coverage removed for their specific conditions. Insurers have also, at times, cancelled a person's insurance when that person has recently made large medical claims or has been diagnosed with a catastrophic disease. The 2010 health legislation makes it illegal for insurance companies to refuse insurance to these people.

Health Insurance Comes of Age

The twentieth century brought important new opportunities for large numbers of people to acquire health insurance. Developments included the creation of nonprofit health insurance companies, employer-sponsored insurance programs, and government programs for older and low-income people.

The lower premiums charged by nonprofit insurers enabled many more people to afford health insurance. The lower premiums resulted from the companies forgoing a profit and insuring large numbers of people. This enabled the companies to obtain contracts for lower rates from hospitals and doctors and to pass these lower rates on to their customers.

By mid-century, strong unions had begun to include health insurance among the benefits they demanded for their members. As a result, many employers began to pay at least part of the cost of health insurance, which lowered the cost for their workers. Also, government programs emerged to cover health insurance costs for many who lacked adequate medical care. Social Security for the disabled, Medicare for the elderly, and Medicaid for those with low incomes gave substantial assistance to large portions of the population. By the century's close, the government was funding half of all health care costs, with individuals and employers funding the other half.

In spite of these government programs, the twenty-first century has seen growing numbers of people with no health insurance or with inadequate insurance. Some Americans lost insurance because they lost their jobs. Some were denied insurance because of previous medical claims or preexisting conditions. Some people, although they were not living in poverty, could no longer afford the rising insurance premiums. The call for government action could not be ignored.

A Determined President Faces the Challenge

Many political leaders were convinced Congress would not pass health legislation in 2010, but President Barack Obama and others were determined to enact a plan. The administration favored reform that would enable virtually everyone to be enrolled in a health plan. When speaking about health care to the joint houses of Congress, President Obama said, "I am not the first president to take up this cause, but I am determined to be the last."

President Obama's hope of solving health care problems once and for all may have been unrealistic. However, the resulting plan did remove some major blocks to health care and open the way for millions more people to obtain insurance. Many saw it as a strong and positive step forward.

Some provisions of the 2010 health plan became law right away. Others will be implemented over several years. The following are a few of the significant changes that were scheduled to begin in 2010:

1. Insurance companies will not be allowed to drop people from coverage because of previous illnesses. Nor will insurance companies be allowed to limit the amount they must pay an insured person over a lifetime. In addition, a company's ability to limit payouts in a given year will be restricted.

2. Individuals younger than nineteen with preexisting conditions will be able to obtain insurance. In the past, insurance companies have often refused to insure these patients. Now that is against the law. (Adults with preexisting conditions will be included starting in 2014.)

3. Young adults will be able to remain insured as dependents under their parents' insurance plans until age twenty-six. Previously, young adults could be dropped from their parents' plans when they finished college or when they turned nineteen if they were not in college.

4. Early retirees (those who retire between ages fifty-five and sixty-four) will be able to obtain temporary coverage until they reach age sixty-five, when they can get coverage through Medicare. In the past, younger retirees often lost their employer-based insurance but were not yet eligible for Medicare. As a result, such individuals had to seek expensive private insurance.

5. Senior citizens will get additional help with prescription drug coverage. Prior to 2010, people on the Medicare Plan D prescription drug program had to pay their total prescription costs above $2,510 in a single year until their costs reached $4,050, the level of catastrophic prescription assistance. In 2010, senior citizens will receive a payment of $250

BREAKING NEWS • BREAKING NEWS • BREAKING NEWS • BREAKING NEWS • BREAKING NEWS • BREAKING

President Barack Obama addresses Congress in September 2009 to encourage the adoption of a comprehensive health care plan. Six months later, though Obama's popularity had declined, a plan was enacted.

to compensate for their lack of Medicare assistance in this interval, sometimes called the "doughnut hole." According to the law, the gap will be closed by 50 percent in 2011 and completely eliminated by 2020.

6. Some small businesses will receive a tax credit to help them provide health insurance for their workers.

Changes scheduled for 2011 include Medicare coverage of some preventive health measures, as well as bonus Medicare payments to primary care physicians and general surgeons. By 2014, the new law requires most people to obtain health insurance. A government subsidy will help those with low incomes pay for the insurance. The law also requires each state to set up health benefit exchanges. These are central agencies through which individuals and small businesses can purchase insurance. Many details of the plan will be developed later.

Bitter feelings remain between some who supported the plan and others who opposed it. A look at the contrasting viewpoints will reveal deep differences in beliefs that have persisted in the nation for decades.

CHAPTER 3

GOVERNMENT, INSURANCE, AND THE HEALTH CARE INDUSTRY: WHY CAN'T THEY ALL AGREE?

P residents and members of Congress have struggled for decades with the divisive political issues that surround health care reform. Two fundamental questions have stirred the debate since the late nineteenth century: what role should the federal government play in guaranteeing access to health care? What role should it play in financing health care costs?

In each decade, some have answered that health care is none of the government's business. Others have contended that health care, like police protection, schools, or highways, should be equally available to everyone and publicly financed through taxation.

New proposals have regularly appeared in an attempt to find an approach that all could embrace. At times, there has been general

One of the many presidents who advocated national health care, Theodore Roosevelt spoke to Americans from the back of a train early in the twentieth century.

agreement that a national plan was needed. However, the fate of a proposed plan has often depended on the country's economic state, its national security status, or the popularity of the president in office. All the while, the same basic differences have divided the nation. Even after passage of the 2010 health plan, the heated debate has continued.

A CENTURY OF CONTENTIOUS PROPOSALS

In 1912, Theodore Roosevelt advocated national health insurance in his third-party presidential bid for a third term. The idea of a more progressive government was popular. But with three parties, the movement's strength was divided, and he and his health plan lost.

Two decades later, in the early 1930s, medical costs were rising and sickness had become one of the leading causes of poverty. However, President Franklin D. Roosevelt's support for national health insurance was pushed aside by a long and deep economic depression. National health care was tabled in favor of a jobs program and the creation of Social Security to prevent poverty among the elderly.

President Lyndon B. Johnson signs the Social Security Act Amendments of 1965, which established Medicare, while former president Harry Truman, Lady Bird Johnson, and Bess Truman look on.

One major opponent to a health program was the AMA, which feared that physicians might lose control over the practice of medicine if government became involved. Also opposed were Southern Democrats, who believed a national plan might force more racial integration in medical care facilities.

President Harry Truman's belief in the right to medical care was popular in the 1940s. He supported a single insurance system and subsidies for low-income citizens without government interference with doctors or medical services. But again, Southern Democrats and the AMA blocked the plan by spreading the fear of "socialized medicine."

President Lyndon Johnson's popularity in the 1960s helped push Medicare Parts A and B through Congress to provide health care for senior citizens. Congress also passed Medicaid to provide health care for low-income and disabled citizens. Richard Nixon, who served as president from 1968 to 1974, favored stronger government involvement in health care. However, his personal scandals, along with the AMA's continued objection to socialized medicine, dampened public support.

In the 1980s, President Ronald Reagan's priorities were tax cuts and huge increases in defense spending, both of which increased the nation's debt and prevented the addition of a major health program. Though President Jimmy Carter strongly favored universal health insurance, his administration's focus shifted to holding down medical costs. Universal health insurance was again set aside.

While George H.W. Bush was president, from 1988 to 1992, a variety of health care plans were proposed. He spoke about the need for reform, but favored leaving health care in the hands of private enterprise, or profit-making businesses. As the century ended, President Bill Clinton's administration proposed an ambitious health care plan. Though there was a campaign from the White House for a comprehensive plan, support was splintered by criticism and competing plans. The century ended with no national health plan in place. All the while, medical costs, insurance costs, and the number of uninsured citizens spiraled upward.

COST AND CONTROL: THE GREAT DIVIDE

Today few Americans would object to the goal of creating a health care system that works for everyone. Many people support a national

BREAKING NEWS • BREAKING NEWS • BREAKING NEWS • BREAKING NEWS • BREAKING NEWS • BREAKING

Members of the American Grassroots Coalition and the Tea Party Express demonstrate in opposition to the proposed health care reform bill in Washington, D.C., in March 2010.

plan. Polls taken in 2009 by the Kaiser Family Foundation, *Time*, Grove Insight Opinion Research, the *New York Times*, and *CBS News* all showed many more people in favor of a public health plan than opposed to the idea. However, whenever a particular plan has been proposed, opposition groups have mobilized to protect their own special interests, rather than cooperating to find an approach to health care that works for all. In addition, many citizens have objected to programs that do not fit with their political philosophies.

Objections raised against President Obama's 2010 health plan were similar to those that defeated proposals in past decades. Debates

WHAT ARE HEALTH INSURANCE EXCHANGES?

The health care act signed into law by President Obama in March 2010 requires the creation of state-operated health insurance exchanges, which will open in 2014. A health insurance exchange is an organization through which people may obtain information about health insurance and purchase insurance if they wish. Each exchange will contract with health insurers to offer insurance at reasonable prices. Health insurance exchanges must offer at least two different insurance plans from which to choose.

The exchange program will primarily serve those who do not have access to employer-based health insurance or other appropriate coverage, but any residents may obtain insurance through the exchange in their state. Exchanges will assist residents in enrolling in insurance programs, just as an employer-based plan would do. Employers may also arrange for insurance programs for their employees through the exchanges.

centered on how much the plan would cost and who would be in control of health care.

Some people have objected to greater government involvement in health care. They argue that privately run health care is more efficient and less prone to waste, fraud, and abuse than a public system. Those who oppose public plans also fear that the government, if it gets involved with health care, will interfere with their private lives. Opponents of the 2010 legislation warned that patients would no longer be able to choose their doctors, hospitals, or nursing facilities, though nothing in the plan suggested these possibilities. On the contrary, the plan enables patients who had previously been unable to see a doctor except in an emergency room to seek care from a private doctor or clinic of their own choosing.

Anxiety over the cost of a national health care system has also been behind much of the opposition. Opponents of the 2010 plan predicted an enormous increase in the national debt, which some said could bankrupt the country. In addition, the threat of increased taxes stirred up resentment.

INSURING THE UNINSURED

Though some fear changing the system they know, repeated failure to enact a plan that ensures health care for all has exacted a heavy price on the nation. It has resulted in higher death rates and less desirable health outcomes, with children especially at risk. A 2007 study in *USA Today* reported that uninsured children have poorer outcomes from medical treatment than do insured children.

The use of emergency rooms for routine care by the uninsured adds greatly to the cost of health care. In 2007, the California HealthCare Foundation reported that treatment in an emergency room is three to four times more expensive than a trip to the doctor's office. Also, when emergency room staff and resources are tied up giving routine care, those with real emergencies have longer waits and receive less attention from medical staff.

In addition, a health system in which people are insured and illnesses can be treated early is actually a financial asset. Early treatment costs much less than waiting until illnesses become emergencies requiring surgery, long hospitalizations, or care for lifelong disabilities.

With Medicare insuring people who are too old to work, and Medicaid insuring those with very low incomes, who are the uninsured people who cannot get medical care?

While some members of the Thompson family were able to get health insurance, other members were denied coverage because of preexisting medical conditions. The 2010 law makes such denial illegal.

Many circumstances can cause productive citizens to be uninsured. When a catastrophic illness or serious accident occurs, the resulting costs can quickly exhaust the financial resources of victims, even those who have insurance and savings. Before the 2010 health legislation, an insurance company could cancel insurance when medical costs mounted, leaving the victims uninsured. It could also refuse to insure people with preexisting conditions that put them at higher risk of illness.

Job loss in a recessed economy not only causes victims to lose their income, but often eliminates their source of insurance as well. Illness itself can cause inability to work, resulting in loss of employment and insurance. Often the only jobs readily available in a community pay minimum wage, making it a challenge for workers to feed, clothe, and provide a home for their families. Also, many of these jobs do not provide health insurance. Single parents with very young children frequently find that child-care costs exceed what their income can cover, and purchasing health insurance is not possible. Workers who are laid off from higher-paying, professional jobs must usually pay the full cost of insurance themselves at exorbitant prices that many cannot afford. Large numbers of uninsured citizens fall into one of these categories.

Is the Free Market the Answer?

Many Americans think of the United States as a competitive, free enterprise nation in which profit is the measure of success and the motivation for achievement. Some of them view the business model as the best way to deal with problems of any kind. Most insurance companies, pharmaceutical companies, doctors' offices, and private clinics are profit-making businesses. Some people believe health care should remain a profit-making industry, like automobile manufacturing or electronics. They believe the free market will make the health care system run efficiently. For example, some argue that if Americans had more choices about which private insurance plans they could purchase—such as the ability to buy insurance from other states—insurance companies would have to compete to provide the best care at the lowest prices.

However, others observe that health care businesses work differently from other industries. A person can seldom postpone a doctor visit or surgery until prices come down, as one might postpone buying a new car. Also, a patient must usually accept the amount a doctor or hospital charges and cannot shop around for a cheaper appendectomy or echocardiogram.

Unless regulated by the government, insurance and prescription drug prices are seldom affected by the law of supply and demand as grocery prices are. While free enterprise may work well in some areas, those who support a public health plan believe health care is like education, law enforcement, or the highway system and works best when approached collectively.

CHAPTER 4

ETHICAL DILEMMAS IN HEALTH CARE DECISIONS

Ethics refers to the principles or values by which a person or group makes choices and decisions. For example, there are many ways a person, business, or nation can choose to use money and other resources. The choices they make result from the decision makers' values, or what they believe to be most important.

There are many choices and issues within health care that raise difficult ethical questions. One fundamental question stands at the center of the debate: is health care best managed primarily by profit-making businesses or by government representatives? Another major question concerns how the money and other resources available for health care should be used.

ALLOCATION OF LIMITED RESOURCES

Even when the government provides financial assistance, the money available for health care is always limited. Trained medical staff and expensive technological equipment are also limited in any care facility or community, and the demand for them is great. Questions

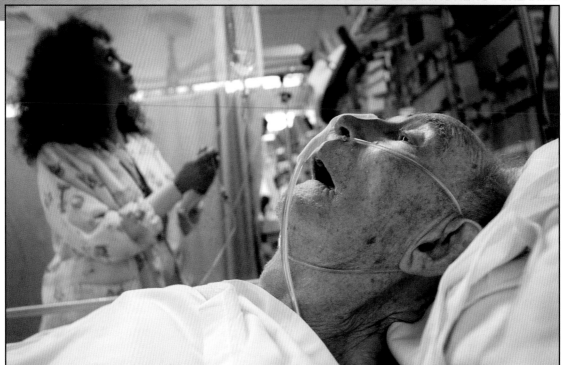

Although most Americans say they would prefer a more natural death, billions of Medicare dollars are spent annually to sustain elderly patients in their final two months of life.

about how medical funds should be spent and how limited resources should be allocated arouse strong emotions whenever leaders attempt to discuss them.

In November 2009, *CBS News* reported that in the previous year, Medicare paid $50 billion for the care of patients in their final two months of life. This is an amount greater than the entire budget of the Department of Homeland Security or the Department of Education. Many terminally ill patients are cared for in intensive care units, where costs are up to $10,000 per day. Often the equipment, such as breathing or feeding tubes keeping a patient alive, is so uncomfortable that patients have to be sedated or restrained. In addition to the cost and the indignity to the patient, critical hospital facilities and staff are busy giving care that often makes little or no improvement in the patient's outlook or comfort.

The majority of Americans express the wish not to spend their last days kept alive artificially by machines and tubes. In addition, many people are interested in finding more natural and comfortable and less costly ways to care for the dying. However, in the recent discussions of health care reform, those who proposed alternative approaches, such as asking people ahead of time about their end-of-life wishes, were accused of wanting to kill older people in order to save money.

Similar emotional debates made headlines in 2005 when the husband of a seriously injured woman, Terri Schiavo, sought legal permission to remove life support machines that had kept her alive long after her brain function had ceased. Some people objected to the removal of life support as equivalent to "playing God," or even to killing, according to their beliefs. Other people felt it was more humane to allow Schiavo to die naturally and peacefully, since she would never return to normal communication, movement, or awareness.

People can have legitimate ethical debates about these issues, and different people may have different answers. However, it is important that Americans learn to discuss the realities and choices related to death and dying without accusations and hysteria.

Many other ethical issues regularly arise in debates over health care spending and the use of resources, such as who should receive organs for transplants when there are more waiting recipients than there are donors. There are ongoing debates about whether government funds

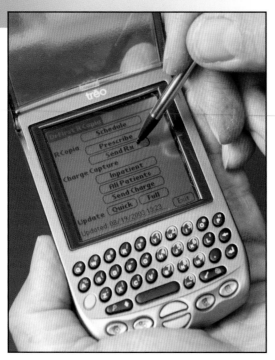

Many Americans rely on prescription drugs, rather than changing their diets and lifestyles. Unnecessary drugs and medical tests increase the cost of health care.

should be available for abortions or for stem cell research. Because not everyone agrees about what values are most important, disagreement on how health resources should be used will continue.

An Ounce of Prevention or a Pound of Cure?

Preventive medicine and health education are areas in which investing additional resources could improve people's quality of life and reduce later medical costs. The 2010 health plan includes funding for several preventive programs. These include individual risk assessments and preventive health plans for Medicare recipients, behavior modification programs to stop smoking and improve diet, and employment-based health programs.

Doctors and patients alike face ethical questions about the use of expensive but unneeded medical tests, technology, and medications. For example, medications such as drugs to lower cholesterol are sometimes necessary. However, at times they are prescribed by doctors or requested by patients when lifestyle changes, such as diet or exercise, would be equally effective. Doctors often find it difficult to educate their patients and persuade them to make the needed lifestyle changes. In addition, insurance companies reward doctors more for treatments than for preventive medicine. But the medications are costly, whereas lifestyle changes cost very little and can often provide additional health benefits.

THE PRICE OF MEDICAL MISTAKES

As the new millennium dawned, the number of serious, avoidable medical errors (malpractice) committed by doctors, hospitals, and other health providers had reached alarming levels. In August 2004, *Medical News Today* reported that across the United States, an average of 195,000 people were dying each year due to preventable medical errors in hospitals. Preventable medical errors include performing unnecessary surgery, negligence in surgery procedures, using incorrect medication or failing to medicate, and failing to use adequate measures to prevent infections. In a single state, New Jersey, 9,400 serious errors were reported in 2007. These errors led patients to develop infections, blood clots, and other dangerous conditions. The associated cost of these tragedies in the United States is estimated to be more than $6 billion per year.

At the same time, the legal problems of doctors and hospitals were also becoming a crisis. In recent years, a large number of malpractice lawsuits have been brought against doctors. Some of them have resulted in enormous monetary awards to patients and families. In 2006, the *New England Journal of Medicine* reported that while approximately three-fourths of malpractice suits were settled without going to court, the average amount awarded in court cases was nearly

Doctors demonstrate in Harrisburg, Pennsylvania, for state legislation to control the cost of medical malpractice lawsuits and insurance.

half a million dollars. As a result, the cost of the malpractice insurance needed by doctors to protect themselves from these judgments had risen to a level many physicians could not afford. Some doctors, especially those in high-risk specialties like obstetrics, chose to close their practices. Others covered the higher costs by charging higher patient fees.

Many more doctors began to practice "defensive medicine," ordering many expensive diagnostic tests that were not really necessary, hoping to protect themselves from malpractice lawsuits. While most

DID YOU KNOW...?

According to the National Academy of Sciences Institute of Medicine, more than a million patients per year suffer injury or death because of avoidable medical errors. About eighty-five thousand medical malpractice lawsuits are brought against doctors, hospitals, and other health providers each year. Below are facts about lawsuits brought against health providers:

- Ninety percent of medical malpractice lawsuits are related to the permanent injury or death of a patient.
- In more than one out of four cases, the lawsuit succeeds against the doctor or other health provider.
- Almost 50 percent of medical malpractice suits are brought against surgeons.
- About 25 percent of all doctors are sued in any given year.
- More than 50 percent of all doctors are sued at least once in their medical careers.

people agree that patients must have the right to sue doctors who have been truly negligent, some people argue that the lawsuits have gotten out of control. Many believe they are also leading to waste in medicine. For example, a doctor may agree to a test simply because a patient requests it, and not because the test is appropriate.

In recent years, many have called for tort reform, that is, reform of the court system that processes malpractice lawsuits. People have called for changes to limit the number of malpractice lawsuits brought to court and to control the sums awarded to patients when health providers are found to be at fault. However, while politicians have made tort reform a big issue in recent campaigns, a 2006 report by the Robert Wood Johnson Foundation notes that the malpractice crisis has not had a great impact on access to medical care or its cost.

A few states have passed laws limiting some types of malpractice judgments and making courts more diligent in filtering out suits that have little merit. Rather than enacting tort reform in the 2010 health care legislation, the Obama administration included funding for five-year demonstration grants with which states can develop, implement, and evaluate tort reform plans.

Much national attention is focused on the plight of doctors and hospitals faced with possible malpractice suits, as well as on controlling the costs involved. However, the *Consumer Reports* "Health" blog reminds us that primary consideration should go to those who suffer and die because of preventable medical errors. According to reporter Kathy Mitchell, the victims of medical malpractice "shouldn't give up their rights until we implement real safety measures that improve the quality of care and reduce errors."

While the 2010 health plan addresses some ethical issues, these issues and others will continue to challenge government, health care providers, and individuals and make headlines whenever they are discussed.

CHAPTER 5

The Future of Health Care

L ike many features of American life, the Patient Protection and Affordable Care Act is a compromise. The plan leaves ownership and operation of insurance companies, pharmaceutical makers, and health care facilities largely in the hands of for-profit businesses and corporations. At the same time, the legislation establishes new government responsibilities, regulations, and funding to ensure that Americans can obtain health care when needed. The coming months and years will reveal whether such a plan can successfully improve health outcomes in the United States. Although the legislation was signed into law, its provisions will be subject to review, revision, and challenges to their constitutionality for some time to come.

CONSTITUTIONAL CHALLENGES

Just as the U.S. attorney general serves as the nation's chief legal adviser, a state attorney general serves that role within each state. Even before the president had signed the 2010 health bill, at least a dozen state attorneys general were already prepared to challenge its constitutionality.

The Claim: The Plan Is Unconstitutional

The challenges to the new legislation came in two major areas. The first stems from the law's requirement that all U.S. citizens and legal residents purchase health insurance beginning in 2014. The law provides financial help for those with incomes too low to afford the insurance. Those challenging the plan claim that the federal government does not have the right to force citizens to buy insurance against their will. Virginia attorney general Ken Cuccinelli argues that, while the federal government can regulate commerce, a person who declines to buy insurance is not engaging in commerce. Therefore, his or her decision cannot be regulated by the government.

The second challenge is based on provisions in the law that place requirements on the states. For example, the plan requires that Medicaid, a state-based health insurance program for low-income families, extend coverage to include categories of people who were not previously eligible. Also, the plan requires states to establish and operate health insurance exchanges and health options programs for small businesses. Furthermore, states must oversee the new programs as they are implemented and operated. Florida attorney general Bill McCollum argues that these requirements infringe on state sovereignty, or the power of the states to govern areas not specifically given to the federal government in the Constitution.

The Claim: The Plan Is Constitutional

Defenders of the legislation respond that the federal government does, in fact, have the right to require Americans to take actions that affect the wider community. For example, the government can require young Americans to register for the draft and serve in the military. The government can require that all Americans pay Social Security and Medicare taxes, which are both forms of insurance.

Whether or not an individual has health insurance does affect the wider community. If an uninsured individual is seriously injured or falls victim to a catastrophic illness, the person will be cared for in an emergency room of a hospital, even though he or she cannot pay the bills. Payment for this care comes

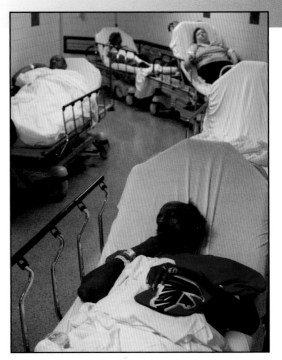

Critically ill patients wait for care in an overcrowded emergency room in Atlanta, Georgia. Uninsured patients seeking routine care in emergency rooms add to the problem.

from several sources, including federal, state, and local public funds, which are all derived ultimately from taxes. The cost is also covered by increasing charges to insured patients. This is a way of involuntarily taxing those who already have insurance. Requiring that everyone purchase health insurance is similar to laws requiring that all drivers be insured. Without this requirement, others must pay the costs of those who choose to remain uninsured.

The attorneys general of some states, such as Richard Cordray of Ohio and Tom Miller of Iowa, have disagreed with the claim that individual health insurance does not affect interstate commerce. At the time the health bill was passed, health care accounted for one-sixth of the U.S. domestic economy. In fact, the rising costs of health care posed basic challenges to the American economic system. This suggests that whether a person has health insurance affects everyone, not just the individual.

THE FUTURE OF HEALTH CARE IN AMERICA

The Urban Institute, a nonpartisan, nonprofit research and educational organization, has estimated the number of uninsured persons in America and the cost of their health care, known as uncompensated care. The organization compared the costs of uncompensated care before implementation of the 2010 law to future estimated costs for this care. The report produced figures for two conditions: first, if the 2010 health care plan is fully implemented, and second, if the plan is not implemented because of repeal or court rulings that the plan is unconstitutional.

In 2009, prior to passage, approximately 49.1 million Americans were uninsured, and the annual cost of uncompensated care had risen to approximately $57.4 billion. Without health care reform, by 2019 the number of uninsured was projected to reach between 57 and 65 million people. The cost of uncompensated care was projected to rise to between $107 billion and $141 billion. On the other hand, if the plan is fully enacted, the number of uninsured individuals is projected to decrease greatly. The cost of uncompensated care will also decrease, in spite of expected rises in health care costs. According to the report, by 2019 the uninsured will have dropped to approximately

Before the 2010 health care legislation, states with the highest numbers of uninsured people, such as California, struggled with the cost of providing basic medical care to residents.

23 million people, and uncompensated care costs to between $36 billion and $46 billion.

In summary, the Urban Institute projects that, without comprehensive health insurance reform, the number of uninsured and the cost of uncompensated health care would continue to grow substantially. As a consequence, pressure on local and state governments to cover uncompensated costs would increase. Also, hospitals and clinics would face increasing financial pressure. In fact, they might not be able to continue to care for the uninsured at the level they currently do.

WHO PAID FOR UNCOMPENSATED CARE BEFORE THE NEW LAW?

Uninsured Americans often need health care, even when they cannot pay. In a 2008 study, the Urban Institute determined who actually paid for that uncompensated care.

Amounts added to Medicare and Medicaid payments to help offset uncompensated care	$ 18.1 billion
Direct care programs (e.g., community health centers, Veterans Health Administration, and Indian Health Service)	$ 14.6 billion
State and local public funds	$ 10.6 billion
Physicians' uncompensated services	$ 7.8 billion
Increased charges to private payers to offset uncompensated care	$ 6.3 billion
Total	$ 57.4 billion

The benefits of a comprehensive health plan extend beyond immediate cost comparisons. Workers' unions initially had to pressure employers into offering health insurance benefits many decades ago. However, employers have continued to offer these benefits because a healthier workforce has proven to be more productive, as are workers who know their children can get health care when needed.

THE MEASURES OF SUCCESS

What is a good health care policy for the country? What should it accomplish? What should Americans look for in the future to measure the success of their health plans?

By passing the Patient Protection and Affordable Care Act in 2010, America took a giant step in a new direction. Still to be determined, though, is whether the legislation can enable America to become a world leader in health outcomes.

No one element characterizes all of the health care programs that have succeeded in other developed countries. While Americans often speak critically of medical care in other countries, especially England and Canada, people who examine those health systems note that they achieve results that have so far eluded the United States. These countries boast equal access to health care for all and far lower costs than in the United States. They also have better health outcomes, such as greater average life spans and lower infant mortality (death rates).

Great Britain has a national health care system in which the government directly employs most doctors. Canada has a centralized single payer system in which everyone is directly insured by the government. Private insurance companies play only a minor role. In the Netherlands, people buy health insurance from private carriers, but virtually everyone has insurance. In France, a nonprofit fund provides everyone with insurance, but individuals can buy supplementary insurance if they wish.

In all four countries, as well as in other leading nations, substantial taxes fund the public health programs. Jonathan Cohn, a senior editor for the *New Republic*, surveyed health plans of other countries in 2008. Though he heard a number of complaints, no one wanted to swap his or her country's health care system with the American system. America is very successful in a few areas in which large sums have been allocated to research. For example, the United States does a good job in treating and preventing some types of cancer. However, other countries have achieved more in overall quality and affordability.

As a nation, America consumes more food, uses more energy, buys more cars, and spends more money per person than any other nation. At the same time, in the name of protecting and promoting free enterprise, we have allowed millions of citizens to go without access to medical care. Sharing the urgent concern of many previous presidents, Barack Obama made health care for everyone a top priority in his administration. Though compromises were made, a plan was achieved that will enable 95 percent of Americans to obtain health insurance. The plan is not the perfect answer but a work in progress. The decision makers of tomorrow can evaluate its effectiveness in the coming years and then work for additional changes that will help America become a compassionate leader in health care.

GLOSSARY

allocation Something apportioned or divided for specific purposes.

capitalism An economic system characterized by private ownership and competition in a free market.

defensive medicine The practice of making medical decisions based primarily on the avoidance of lawsuits, rather than therapeutic value.

employer-based insurance An insurance plan made available and subsidized by a person's employer.

ethics The principles or values by which a person or group makes choices.

free enterprise A system in which private businesses operate competitively and for profit, with a minimum of government control.

health insurance exchange A state-based agency through which individuals or employers can obtain information about and purchase health insurance.

insurance claim A request made by an insured person for payment from the insurance provider for a medical service, drug, or device.

insurance premium The amount a person or group must pay an insurance provider to be insured.

Medicaid A health care program financed by federal and state governments for low-income Americans, who otherwise could not afford care.

medical malpractice Avoidable medical errors committed by doctors, hospitals, or other health providers.

Medicare A federal health insurance program for U.S. citizens age sixty-five or older.

obstetrics The branch of medicine that deals with birth.

preexisting condition An illness or medical condition that was diagnosed or treated before enrollment in a new health insurance plan.

preventive medicine Actions taken by health providers and patients to maintain good health and prevent illness.

primary care provider A doctor or group of health providers who treat a wide range of illnesses and conditions.

robotics The design and production of machines that can perform some of the functions of humans.

single payer system A system in which a single government-run organization collects all health care fees and pays out all health care costs.

Social Security A government-run insurance program designed to provide income for the elderly in the United States.

terminal illness An illness from which the patient is expected to die.

tort reform Changing the legal system to avoid unnecessary malpractice lawsuits and to make the amounts of money awarded by courts more reasonable.

universal health care A government-run system that ensures health care coverage for all.

FOR MORE INFORMATION

Center for Studying Health System Change

600 Maryland Avenue SW, Suite 550

Washington, DC 20024

(202) 484-5261

Web site: http://www.hschange.com

The Center for Studying Health System Change researches and
publishes information about all aspects of health issues to provide
insights that contribute to better health policy.

Families USA

1201 New York Avenue NW, Suite 1100

Washington, DC 20005

(202) 628-3030

Web site: http://www.familiesusa.org

Families USA is a nonprofit, nonpartisan organization dedicated to
achieving high-quality, affordable health care for all Americans.
Families USA works at the national, state, and community levels.

Health Canada

Address Locator 0900C2

Ottawa, ON K1A 0K9

Canada

(866) 225-0709

Web site: http://www.hc-sc.gc.ca

Health Canada is a federal department that helps Canadians to
maintain and improve their health.

Kaiser Family Foundation

2400 Sand Hill Road

Menlo Park, CA 94025

(650) 854-9400

Web site: http://www.kff.org

The Kaiser Family Foundation is a nonprofit, private foundation that
focuses on the major health care issues facing the United States, as
well as the United States' role in global health policy.

Public Health Agency of Canada

130 Colonnade Road

A. L. 6501H

Ottawa, ON K1A 0K9

Canada

(866) 225-0709

Web site: http://www.publichealth.gc.ca

The Public Health Agency of Canada works to strengthen the country's capacity to protect and improve the health of Canadians. The
agency provides current information about diseases, nutrition, and
other health issues.

U.S. Department of Health and Human Services (HHS)

200 Independence Avenue SW

Washington, DC 20201

(877) 696-6775

Web site: http://www.hhs.gov

The U.S. Department of Health and Human Services is responsible
for protecting the health of Americans and deals with such issues
as aging, children and families, and disease prevention.

World Health Organization

Avenue Appia 20

1211 Geneva 27

Switzerland

Web site: http://www.who.int

The World Health Organization is a specialized agency of the United
Nations that coordinates international public health activities and
provides data and information related to world health issues.

WEB SITES

Due to the changing nature of Internet links, Rosen Publishing has
developed an online list of Web sites related to the subject of this book.
This site is updated regularly. Please use this link to access the list:

http://www.rosenlinks.com/hls/heal

Callahan, Daniel. *Taming the Beloved Beast: How Medical Technology Costs Are Destroying Our Health Care System.* Princeton, NJ: Princeton University Press, 2009.

Cohn, Jonathan. *Sick: The Untold Story of America's Health Care Crisis—and the People Who Pay the Price.* New York, NY: HarperCollins Publishers, 2007.

Daschle, Thomas, Scott S. Greenberger, and Jeanne M. Lambrew. *Critical: What We Can Do About the Health-Care Crisis.* New York, NY: Thomas Dunne Books, 2008.

Davidson, Stephen M. *Still Broken: Understanding the U.S. Health Care System.* Stanford, CA: Stanford Business Books, 2010.

Forman, Lillian E. *Health Care Reform* (Essential Viewpoints). Edina, MN: ABDO, 2010.

Gerdes, Louise I. *Medicine* (Opposing Viewpoints Series). Detroit, MI: Greenhaven Press, 2008.

Haugen, David M. *Health Care* (Opposing Viewpoints Series). Detroit, MI: Greenhaven Press/Gale, 2008.

Hunnicutt, Susan. *Universal Health Care* (Opposing Viewpoints Series). Detroit, MI: Greenhaven Press, 2010.

Kellerman, Faye, and Aliza Kellerman. *Prism.* New York, NY: HarperCollins Publishers, 2009.

Kotlikoff, Laurence J. *The Healthcare Fix: Universal Insurance for All Americans.* Cambridge, MA: MIT Press, 2007.

Kowalski, Kathiann M. *National Health Care* (Open for Debate). New York, NY: Michael Cavendish Benchmark, 2009.

Merino, Noël. *Health Care* (Introducing Issues with Opposing Viewpoints). Detroit, MI: Greenhaven Press, 2010.

Naden, Corinne J. *Health Care: A Right or a Privilege* (Controversy!). Tarrytown, NY: Marshall Cavendish Benchmark, 2010.

Naden, Corinne J. *Patients' Rights* (Open for Debate). New York, NY: Marshall Cavendish Benchmark, 2008.

Parks, Peggy J. *Health Care* (Compact Research Series). San Diego, CA: ReferencePoint Press, 2009.

Reid, T. R. *The Healing of America: A Global Quest for Better, Cheaper, and Fairer Health Care*. New York, NY: Penguin Press, 2009.

Richmond, Julius B., and Rashi Fein. *The Health Care Mess: How We Got Into It and What It Will Take to Get Out*. Cambridge, MA: Harvard University Press, 2005.

Sered, Susan Starr, and Rushika J. Fernandopulle. *Uninsured in America: Life and Death in the Land of Opportunity*. Berkeley, CA: University of California Press, 2005.

Sherrow, Victoria. *Universal Healthcare* (Point-Counterpoint). New York, NY: Chelsea House, 2009.

Shi, Leiyu, and Douglas A. Singh. *Essentials of the U.S. Health Care System*. 2nd ed. Sudbury, MA: Jones and Bartlett Publishers, 2010.

BIBLIOGRAPHY

Altman, Alex. "Are Legal Challenges to Health Reform Credible?" March 23, 2010. Retrieved May 3, 2010 (http://swampland.blogs.time. com/2010/03/23/are-legal-challenges-to-health-reform-credible).

American Academy of Family Physicians. "Charts and Graphs— Media Center." 2010. Retrieved April 9, 2010 (http://www.aafp. org/online/en/home/media/charts-and-graphs.html).

CBSNews.com. "The Cost of Dying" *60 Minutes,* November 22, 2009. Retrieved April 30, 2010 (http://www.cbsnews.com/ stories/2009/11/09/60minutes/main5711689.shtml).

Cohen, Thomas H. "Medical Malpractice Trials and Verdicts in Large Counties, 2001." Bureau of Justice Statistics, April 18, 2004. Retrieved May 2, 2010 (http://bjs.ojp.usdoj.gov/index. cfm?ty=pbdetail&iid=784).

Cohn, Jonathan. "Healthy Examples: Plenty of Countries Get Healthcare Right." *Boston Globe*, July 5, 2009. Retrieved April 5, 2010 (http://www.boston.com/bostonglobe/ideas/articles/2009/07/ 05/healthy_examples_plenty_of_countries_get_healthcare_right).

Congressional Budget Office. "Technological Change and the Growth of Health Care Spending." January 2008. Retrieved April 5, 2010 (http://www.cbo.gov/doc.cfm?index=8947).

Cordray, Richard, and Tom Miller. "Why We Won't File States' Rights Suits." Politico.com, April 2, 2010. Retrieved May 3, 2010 (http://www.politico.com/news/stories/0410/35335.html).

Guardian.co.uk. "How Does US Healthcare Compare to the Rest of the World?" March 22, 2010. Retrieved April 5, 2010 (http://guardian.co.uk/news/datablog/2010/mar/22/ us-healthcare-bill-rest-of-world-obama).

Holahan, John, and Bowen Garrett. "The Cost of Uncompensated Care with and Without Health Reform." Urban Institute, March 2010. Retrieved April 22, 2010 (www.urban.org/ UploadedPDF/412045_cost_of_uncompensated.pdf).

Hoskins, David. "The Impact of Technology on Health Delivery and Access." *Workers World*, December 23, 2009. Retrieved April 5, 2010 (http://www.workers.org/2009/us/sickness_1231).

Intuitive Surgical. "Presentation to the Congressional Robotics Caucus." May 2009. Retrieved April 9, 2010 (http://www.us-robotics.us/presentations/Medical-pdf).

Isaacs, S. L., P. S. Jellinek, and W. L. Ray. "The Independent Physician— Going, Going..." *New England Journal of Medicine*, Vol. 360, No. 7, February 12, 2009. Reprinted by NEJM CareerCenter, March– April 2009. Retrieved April 9, 2010 (http://www.nejmjobs.org/rpt/ independent-physician.aspx).

Kaiser Family Foundation. "Summary of New Health Reform Law." March 2010. Retrieved April 1, 2010 (http://www.kff.org/ healthreform/upload/8061.pdf).

Kaiser Family Foundation. "Trends and Indicators in the Changing Health Care Marketplace: Section Six." 2005. Retrieved April 9, 2010 (www.kff.org/insurance/7031/print-sec6.cfm).

Kelleher, Elizabeth. "Telemedicine's Advantages for Remote Areas: Remote Medicine Using New Technology Can Save Money and Lives." Suite101.com, November 13, 2009. Retrieved April 5, 2010 (http://internet.suite101.com/article.cfm/ telemedicines_advantages_for_remote_areas).

Lepore, Jill. "Preexisting Condition." *New Yorker*, December 7, 2009. Retrieved April 1, 2010 (http://www.newyorker.com/talk/ comment/2009/12/07/091207taco_talk_lepore).

McCarthy, Kevin. "Would Medical Malpractice Reform Fix Our Health-Care System?" March 5, 2010. Retrieved July 13, 2010 (http://blogs.consumerreports.org/health/2010/03/ would-medical-malpractice-reform-fix-our-health-care-system).

McRoberts, Robert. "U.S. Presidents and Health Care Reform: The History of Public Health Politics in America." Suite101.com, September 10, 2009. Retrieved April 14, 2010 (http://modern-us-history.suite101.com/article.cfm/ us_presidents_and_healthcare_reform).

Newport, Frank, and Elizabeth Mendes. "About One in Six U.S. Adults Are Without Health Insurance." Gallup.com, July 22, 2009. Retrieved April 5, 2010 (http://www.gallup.com/poll/121820/one- in-six-adults-without-health-insurance.aspx).

Northern California Neurosurgery Medical Group. "The History of Health Insurance in the United States." November 10, 2009. Retrieved April 1, 2010 (http://www.neurosurgical.com/medi- cal_history_and_ethics/history/history_of_health_ insurance.htm).

New York Times. "Malpractice and Health Care Reform." June 16, 2009. Retrieved May 1, 2010 (http://www.nytimes.com/2009/ 06/17/opinion/17wed2.html).

Physicians for a National Health Program. "What Is Single Payer?" January 11, 2010. Retrieved April 15, 2010 (http://www.pnhp.org/print/facts/what-is-single-payer).

State of California. "Get the Facts: Emergency Care." 2007. Retrieved April 20, 2010 (http://www.fixourhealthcare.ca.gov/index.php/facts/more/6771).

Walker, Forrest A. "Compulsory Health Insurance: The Next Great Step in Social Legislation." *Journal of American History*, Vol. 56, No. 2, September 1969, pp. 290–304. Retrieved April 10, 2010 (http://www.jstor.org/pss/1908125).

Western PA Coalition for Single-Payer Healthcare. "Single-Payer Poll, Survey, and Initiative Results." Retrieved April 22, 2010 (http://www.wpasinglepayer.org/pollresults.html).

Williams, Claudia H., and Michelle M. Mello. "What Is a Medical Malpractice Crisis, and Are We in One?" Robert Wood Johnson Foundation Policy Brief No. 10, May 2006.

Wolf, Richard. "Study: Uninsured Kids Fare Worse at Hospitals." USAToday.com, March 2, 2007. Retrieved April 22, 2010 (http://www.usatoday.com/news/health/2007-03-01-uninsured-kids_x.htm).

World Health Organization. "World Health Statistics 2009." Retrieved April 8, 2010 (http://www.who.int/whosis/whostat/EN_WHS09_Full.pdf).

INDEX

ABOUT THE AUTHOR

Molly Jones writes on health and contemporary issues and is the author of four books and several magazine articles for children and young adults. She has a Ph.D. in educational research and has completed graduate study in epidemiology and biostatistics. Her research has been published in *Medical Care*, *Remedial and Special Education*, and *Journal of Early Intervention*. She lives on Lake Murray near Columbia, South Carolina.

PHOTO CREDITS

Cover, pp. 23, 29 Jewel Samad/AFP/Getty Images; pp. 4–5 Win McNamee/Getty Images; p. 8 Daniel Berehulaak/Getty Images; p. 11 Richard Price/Taxi/Getty Images; p. 16 © North Wind/North Wind Picture Archives; p. 18 Hemera/Thinkstock; p. 26 Fotosearch/Getty Images; p. 27 © Francis Miller/Time & Life Pictures/Getty Images; pp. 32, 40, 47 © AP Images; p. 36 Mario Tama/Getty Images; p. 38 Alex Wong/Getty Images; p. 45 Jonathan Torgovnik/Edit by Getty Images; interior graphics © www.istockphoto.com/Chad Anderson (globe), © www.istockphoto.com/ymgerman (map), © www.istockphoto.com/Brett Lamb (satellite dish).

Editor: Andrea Sclarow; Photo Researcher: Marty Levick